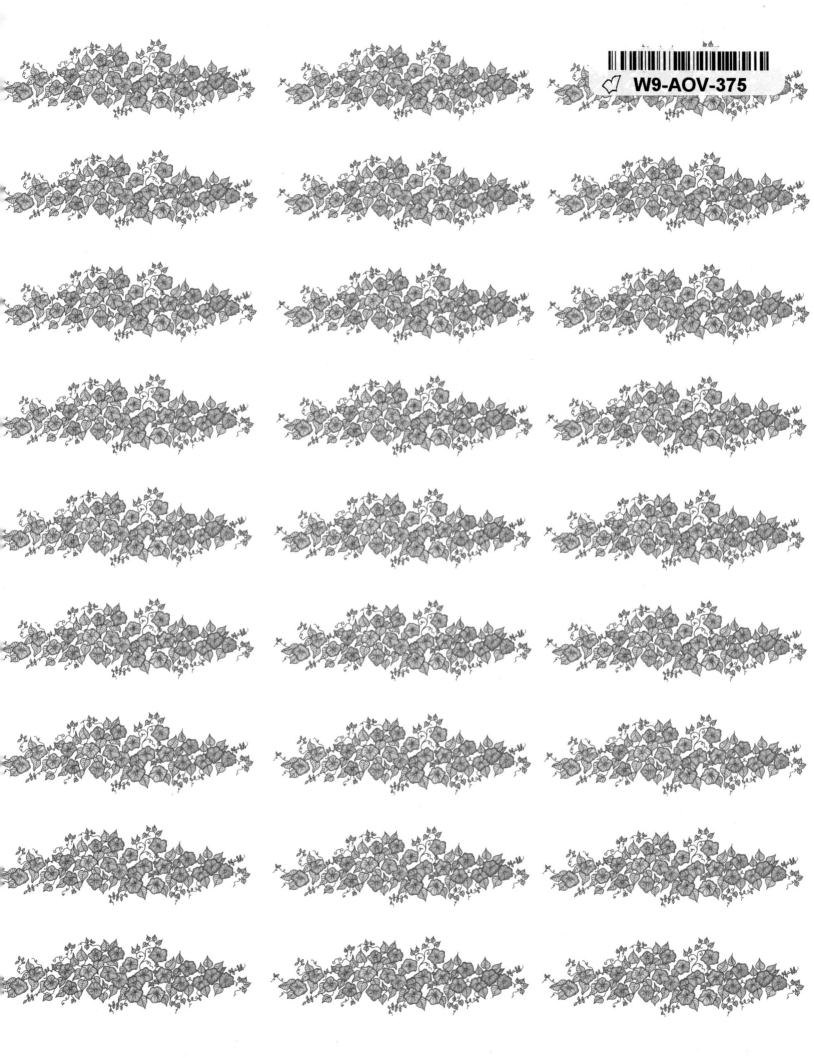

Grandmother's Memories

Elizabeth Loonan

ILLUSTRATIONS BY JANE KENDALL

MetroBooks

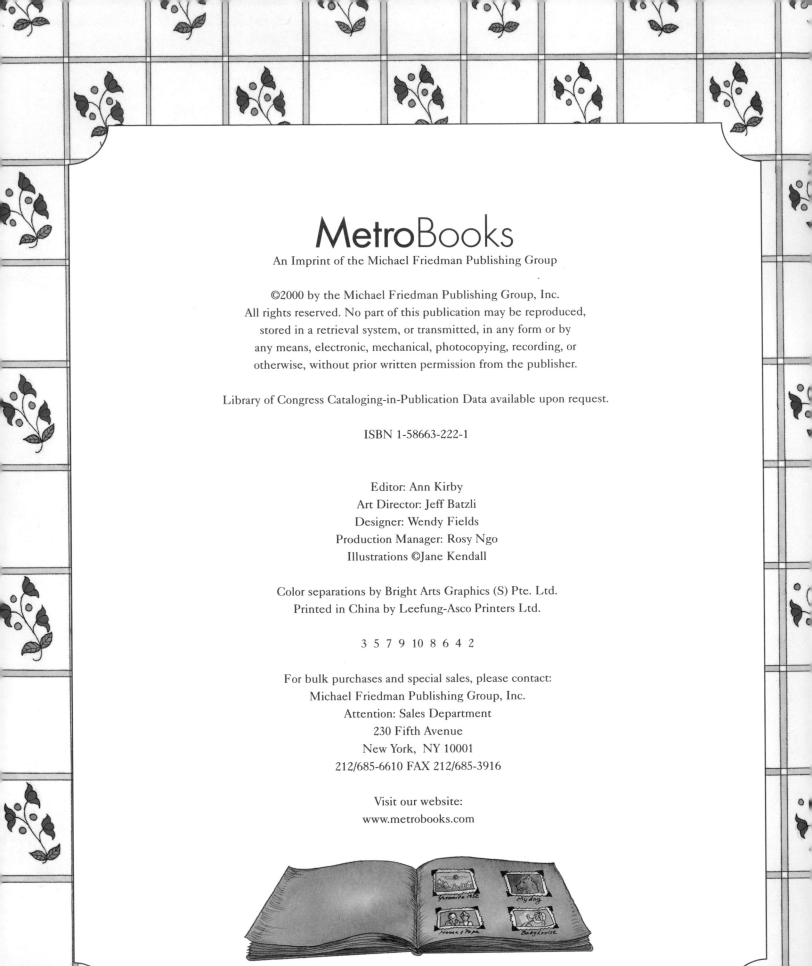

MetroBooks

An Imprint of the Michael Friedman Publishing Group

©2000 by the Michael Friedman Publishing Group, Inc.

Library of Congress Cataloging-in-Publication Data available upon request.

ISBN 1-58663-222-1

Editor: Ann Kirby
Art Director: Jeff Batzli
Designer: Wendy Fields
Production Manager: Rosy Ngo
Illustrations ©Jane Kendall

Color separations by Bright Arts Graphics (S) Pte. Ltd.
Printed in China by Leefung-Asco Printers Ltd.

3 5 7 9 10 8 6 4 2

For bulk purchases and special sales, please contact:
Michael Friedman Publishing Group, Inc.
Attention: Sales Department
230 Fifth Avenue
New York, NY 10001
212/685-6610 FAX 212/685-3916

Visit our website:
www.metrobooks.com

Dedication

This book is written just for you. I have created it so that you will always have a record of my memories. Every day as you grow up you will learn more and more about what it means to be a member of our family. I want you to realize how important it is to know about our heritage, because learning about the past will help you look toward the future. I want to share with you special moments and memories from my own past, as well as memories handed down to me from the generations that came before you. I also want to share meaningful events of the recent past, including examples of how you have enriched my life. As you read through my memories, think about your part in this wonderful family. Above all else, remember how much I love you.

To my dear Grandchild, _____

From your loving Grandmother, _____

Date _____

Contents

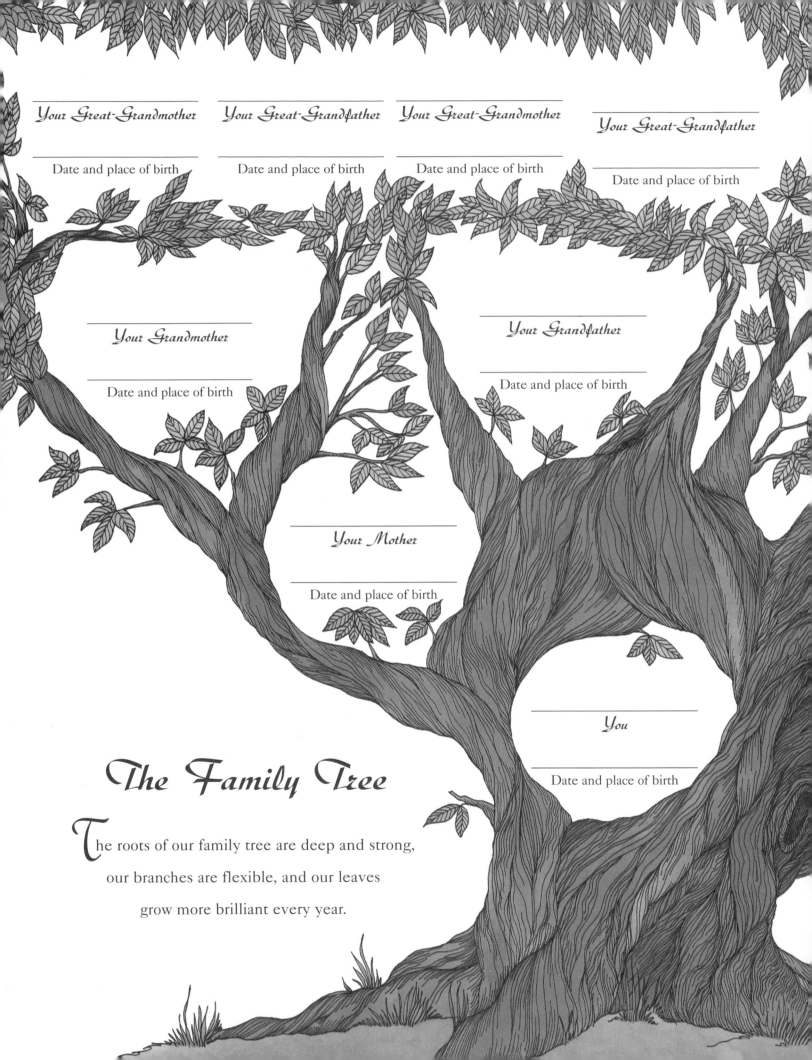

Your Great-Grandmother

Date and place of birth

Your Great-Grandfather

Date and place of birth

Your Great-Grandmother

Date and place of birth

Your Great-Grandfather

Date and place of birth

Your Grandmother

Date and place of birth

Your Grandfather

Date and place of birth

Your Mother

Date and place of birth

You

Date and place of birth

The Family Tree

The roots of our family tree are deep and strong,

our branches are flexible, and our leaves

grow more brilliant every year.

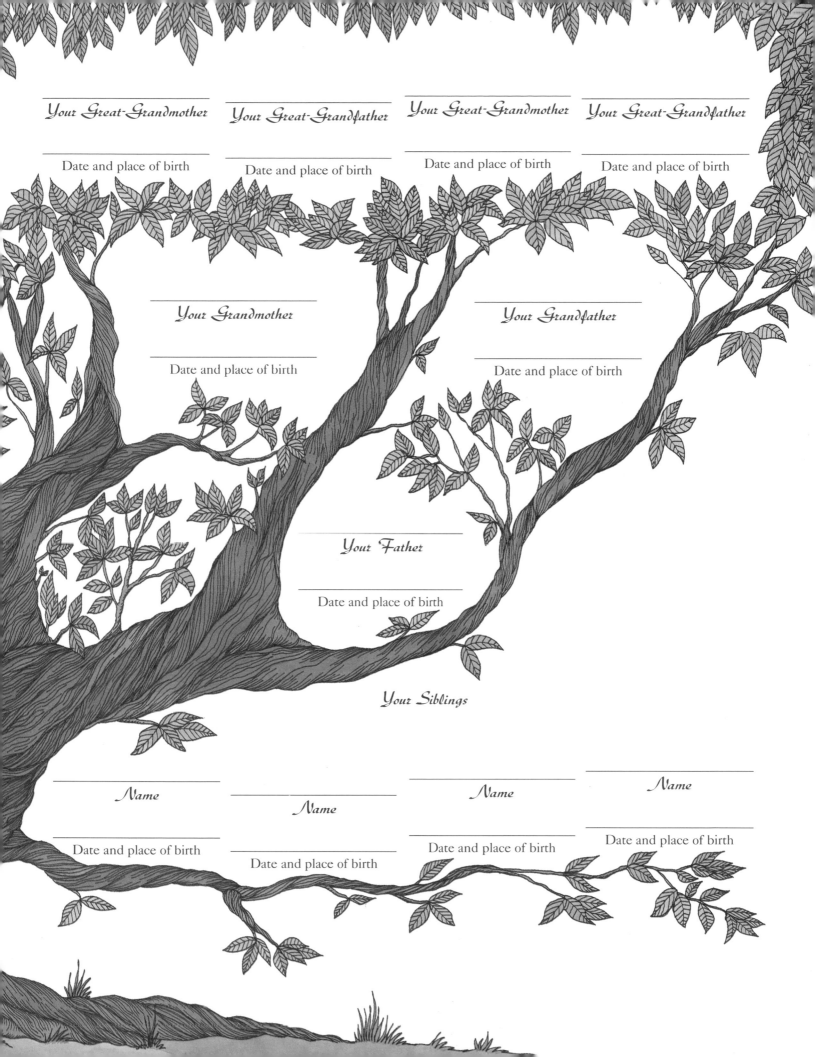

Your Great-Grandmother

Date and place of birth

Your Great-Grandfather

Date and place of birth

Your Great-Grandmother

Date and place of birth

Your Great-Grandfather

Date and place of birth

Your Grandmother

Date and place of birth

Your Grandfather

Date and place of birth

Your Father

Date and place of birth

Your Siblings

Name

Date and place of birth

Name

Date and place of birth

Name

Date and place of birth

Name

Date and place of birth

Memories of My Grandparents— Your Great-Great-Grandparents

My Mother's Family

My grandmother's name was _____

She was born in _____

Her family originally came from _____

My grandfather's name was _____

He was born in _____

His family originally came from _____

My grandparents married in _____

They had _____ children, _____

_____

They lived in _____

My mother told me that my grandparents _____

_____

I remember _____

_____

My Father's Family

My grandmother's name was _____

She was born in _____

Her family originally came from _____

My grandfather's name was _____

He was born in _____

His family originally came from _____

My grandparents married in _____

They had _____ children, _____

_____

They lived in _____

My father told me that my grandparents _____

_____

I remember _____

_____

Memories of My Mother—
Your Great-Grandmother

My mother's name was _____

Her birth date was _____

She met my father _____

_____

When I was young, her days were spent _____

_____

At that time, she looked _____

_____

One of the things I loved most about my mother was _____

_____

I also want to tell you _____

_____

_____

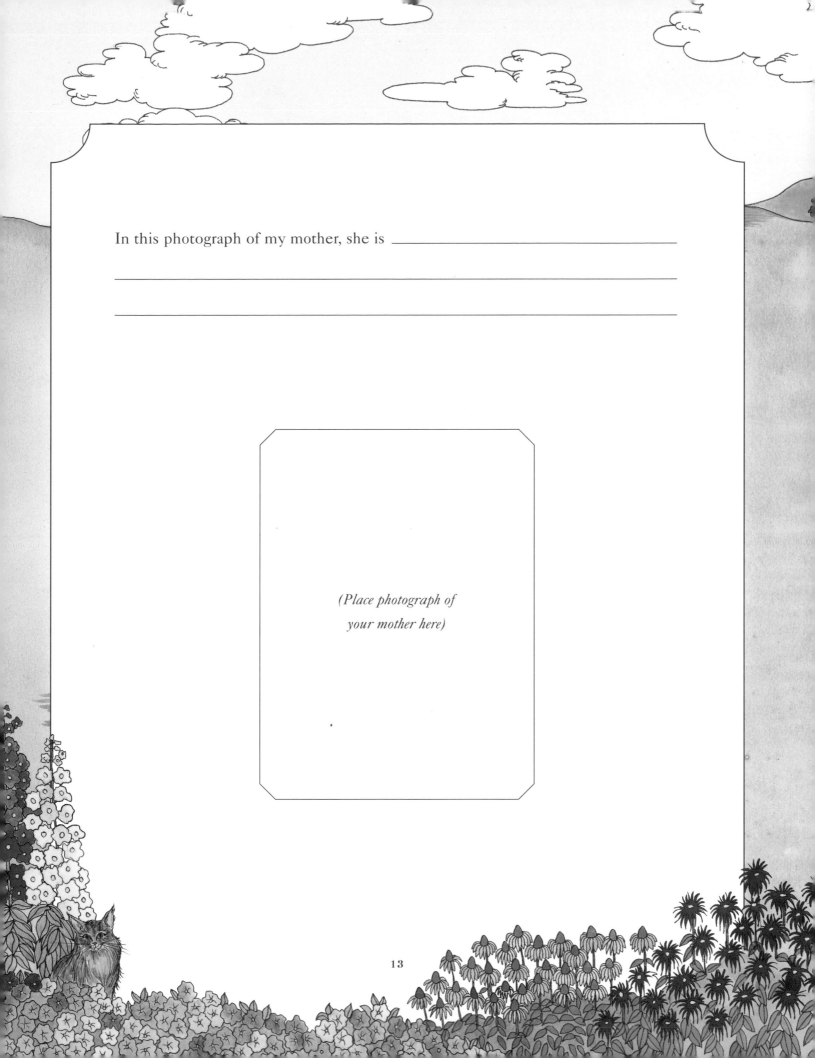

In this photograph of my mother, she is _____

_____

_____

*(Place photograph of
your mother here)*

13

Memories of My Father—
Your Great-Grandfather

My father's name was _____

His birth date was _____

His occupation was _____

He proposed to my mother _____

My parents were married _____

When I was young, he looked _____

One of the things I loved most about my father was _____

_____

_____

I also want to tell you _____

_____

In this photograph of my father, he is _____

_____

_____

*(Place photograph of
your father here)*

When I Was Born

I was born on _____

My birthplace was _____

My full name was _____

My parents named me that because _____

My parents said that when I was born, _____

_____

The earliest memory I have is _____

_____

In this photograph, I am _____ years old. In it, _____

_____

*(Place photograph of
yourself as an infant here)*

My Childhood

When I was a child, I lived in _____

I had _____ siblings, _____

What I loved most about my home was _____

_____

My room was _____

My favorite color was _____

My favorite toy was _____

Pets that I had included _____

_____

Everyone called me _____

When I grew up, I wanted to be _____

My parents used to say I was _____

_____

One of the things I most remember about my childhood is _____

_____

_____

In this photograph, you see _____

(Place photograph from your childhood here)

19

My Youth

I went to school _____

My favorite subject was _____

As a student, I _____

_____

_____

I was also interested in _____

_____

_____

_____

My best friends were _____

_____

_____

_____

_____

_____

_____

We liked to _____

_____

_____

_____

My favorite radio/television program was _____

_____

My favorite song was _____

My favorite movie was _____

My favorite book was _____

I didn't like _____

_____

_____

My most embarrassing moment was _____

_____

_____

_____

_____

_____

Memories of My Family

My parents taught me _____

_____

At home, I was responsible for _____

My favorite family vacation was _____

My favorite holiday was _____

_____

_____

_____

Other relatives who were important to me were _____

_____

_____

_____

I am proud of my family when I remember _____

_____

_____

In this photograph, you see _____

(Place photograph of your family
when you were young here)

When I Was a Young Woman

I was very good at _____

The style of clothing then was _____

My first date was _____

My favorite entertainment was _____

The place I most loved to be was _____

I graduated from _____ High School in 19__. After that, I _____

_____

My favorite job was _____

On the weekends, I _____

_____

_____

A world event that was very meaningful to me at this time was _____

_____

_____

_____

_____

An important thing I accomplished during this period was _____

_____

(Place photograph here)

I Met Your Grandfather

The first time I saw your grandfather was in 19___. He _____

_____

When we met, I was _____

We met because _____

Our first date was _____

I was attracted to him because _____

Our favorite thing to do together was _____

My parents thought he was _____

When I met his parents for the first time, I _____

_____

Here is a memento from our courtship. This is special to me because _____

_____

*(Place photograph or
keepsake here)*

All about Your Grandfather

Grandfather's full name is _____

His birth date is _____

He was born in _____

He had _____ siblings, _____

Grandfather's family came from _____

He grew up in _____

His education was _____

His occupation was _____

Grandfather's favorite pastime was _____

He was very good at _____

Among the things I loved most about him were _____

_____

I remember _____

_____

_____

_____

(Place photograph here)

We Got Engaged

Grandfather asked me to marry him _____

_____

The words he used were _____

_____

My reaction was _____

_____

When we told our families, _____

_____

_____

We announced our betrothal to everyone _____

_____

We celebrated by _____

_____

_____

_____

_____

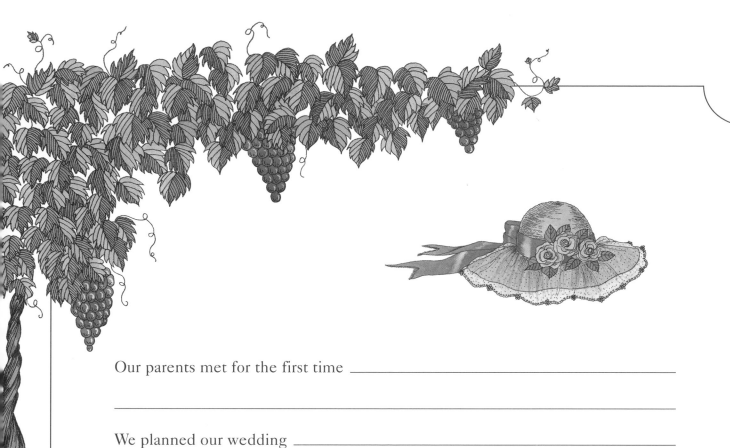

Our parents met for the first time _____

_____

We planned our wedding _____

This photograph was taken _____

*(Place photograph from
your engagement here)*

Memories of Our Wedding

Our wedding took place on _____

The ceremony was _____

I wore _____

Grandfather looked _____

I remember feeling _____

The people we asked to be in our wedding party were _____

_____

Other guests attending the wedding included _____

_____

_____

Our reception was _____

_____

I can remember _____

_____

My favorite things about that day were _____

_____

We honeymooned in _____

In this photograph, we _____

_____

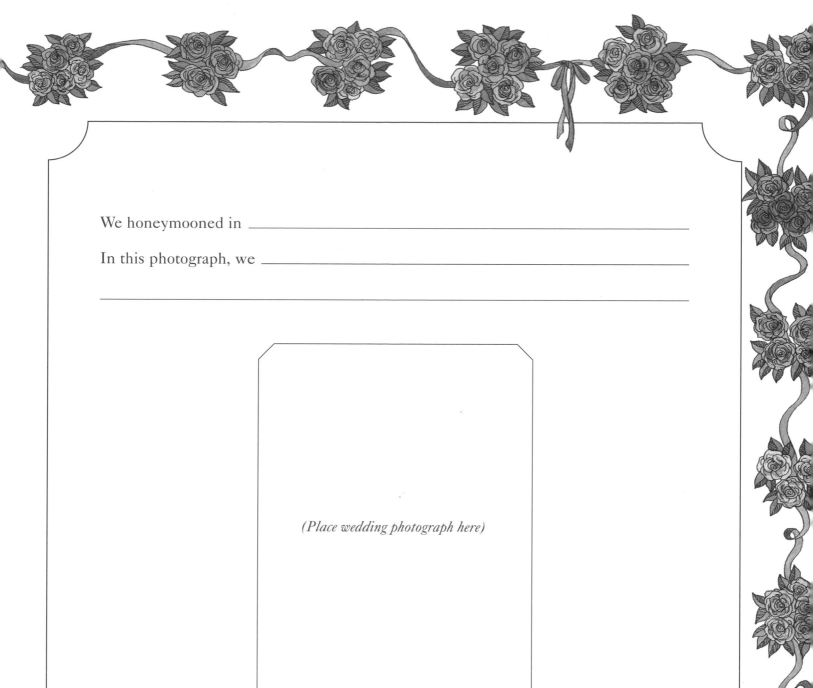

(Place wedding photograph here)

Memories of Our Marriage

Our first home was _____

What I loved most about it was _____

_____

_____

During the day, I _____

_____

_____

Your grandfather _____

_____

In our leisure time, we liked to _____

_____

_____

_____

For our first anniversary, we _____

_____

_____

_____

Our first year of marriage was wonderful, because _____

_____

_____

Our first year of marriage was also difficult, because _____

_____

_____

Our first vacation together was _____

_____

_____

Among our happiest moments were _____

_____

_____

_____

_____

_____

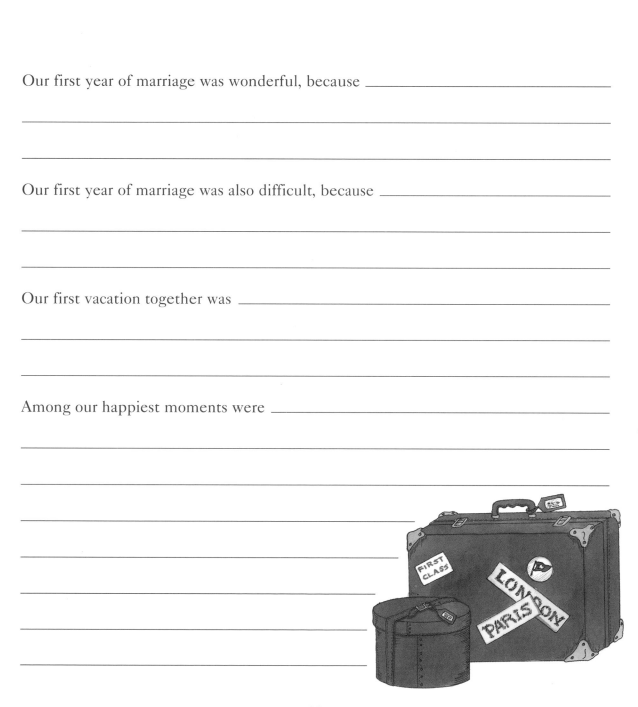

When Your Parent Was Born

When I knew I was expecting, I felt _____

Your parent was born on _____

Your parent's place of birth was _____

We named your parent _____

We chose that name because _____

At birth, your parent was _____

_____

The first thing I said when I saw my baby was _____

_____

I remember your grandfather said _____

_____

I recall feeling _____

We celebrated the new arrival by _____

_____

When talking about your parent's birth, we always say _____

_____

_____

In this photograph, _____

_____

(Place photograph of your child
as an infant here)

Your Parent's Childhood

Your parent has _____ siblings, _____

_____

Your parent's first word was _____

Your parent's first steps were _____

My favorite pet name for your parent was _____

The thing we most liked to do together was _____

I was really surprised when _____

Your parent could not be separated from _____

_____

I'll never forget _____

Other family members thought _____

My favorite story about your parent is _____

_____

_____

_____

I love this photograph because _____

*(Place photograph of
your child here)*

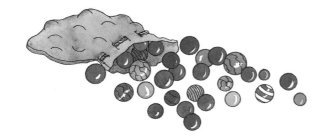

Your Parent's Youth

Your parent went to elementary school at _____

Your parent's favorite subject was _____

Your parent disliked _____

Your parent's nickname was _____

After school your parent _____

_____

Your parent's chores were _____

Your parent's hobby was _____

Your parent's friends were _____

In those days, the style of clothing was _____

_____

The biggest fad of the time was _____

The popular music was _____

The favorite dance was _____

I remember your parent got in trouble when _____

_____

Here's a memento from your parent's school days.

*(Place photograph or
keepsake here)*

When Your Parent Was a Young Adult

Your parent began dating _____

Your parent's first job was _____

The first time your parent went on a trip alone, _____
_____

Your parent graduated from _____ High School in 19___.

After that, your parent _____
_____
_____

Your parent wanted a career as _____

Some of your parent's favorite pastimes were _____
_____

Your parent was also interested in _____

The most important thing I taught your parent was _____
_____

I was so proud of your parent when _____

_____

In this photograph you see _____

_____

(Place photograph of your child
as a young adult here)

When Your Parents Met

Your parents were _____ and _____ years old when they met.

They met because _____

What they said they liked about each other was _____

_____

We all met each other _____

Grandfather and I thought _____

This photograph was taken _____

*(Place photograph of
the young couple here)*

All about Your Other Parent

Full name _____

Birth date _____

Birth place _____

Mother's full name _____

Father's full name _____

Names of siblings _____

Family heritage _____

Education _____

Occupation _____

Hobbies _____

Activities _____

Memories of
Your Parents' Courtship

Your parents dated for _____

They used to love to _____

_____

Grandfather and I knew they were in love when _____

_____

They became engaged _____

_____

The story they tell about it is _____

_____

_____

The first thing I said when I heard was _____

_____

_____

_____

_____

I remember feeling _____

_____

_____

We celebrated by _____

_____

_____

When I met your other grandparents for the first time, _____

_____

_____

I'll never forget _____

_____

_____

_____

_____

_____

When Your Parents Married

The date of their marriage was _____

The ceremony took place at _____

Your mother wore _____

Your father wore _____

They looked _____

Their attendants were _____

_____

_____

Also attending the wedding were _____

_____

_____

_____

The reception was _____

_____

I remember feeling _____

_____

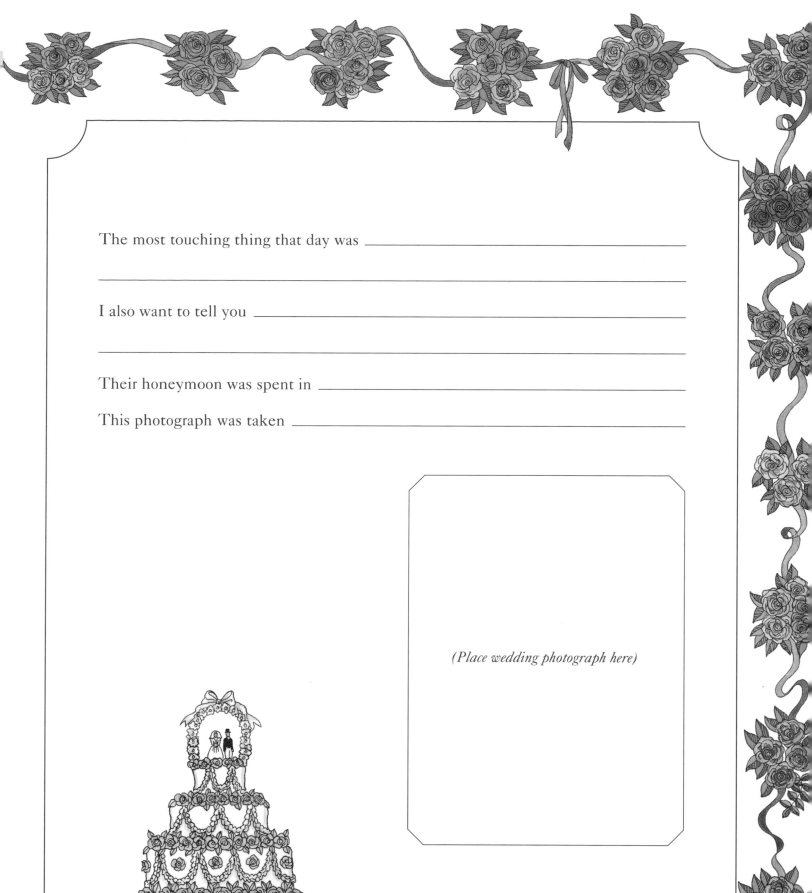

The most touching thing that day was _____

_____

I also want to tell you _____

_____

Their honeymoon was spent in _____

This photograph was taken _____

(Place wedding photograph here)

You Were Born

When I heard your mother was expecting, I _____

_____

Your birth date is _____

You were born in _____

You weighed _____ , and you were _____ long.

Your name was chosen because _____

I heard about your birth _____

At the moment I heard, I was _____

The first thing I said was _____

I also remember _____

My favorite story about your birth is _____

This photograph was taken when you were _____

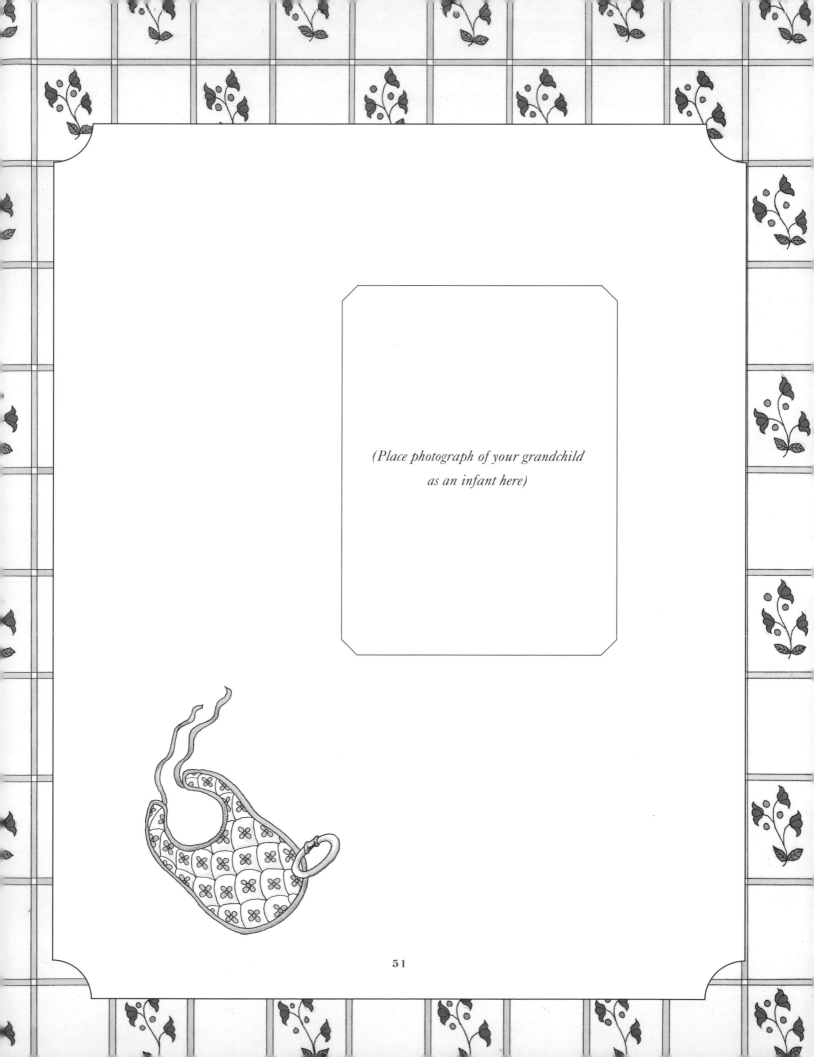

(Place photograph of your grandchild
as an infant here)

51

All about You

You were the type of infant who _____

Your first word was _____

You took your first steps at the age of _____

You reminded me of _____

Your favorite song when you were a baby was _____

Your favorite game was _____

Your favorite toy was _____

At bedtime you _____

You showed me how smart you are when _____

_____

I was very proud of you when _____

_____

On your first birthday, _____

_____

I remember I gave you _____

I'll never forget _____

_____

I love this photograph because _____

(Place photograph of
your grandchild here)

My Favorite Things about Being Your Grandmother

The first time I saw you, _____

I thought you looked like _____

I always smile when you _____

On your first visit to me, _____

Spending time with you is _____

_____

The story I love to tell my friends about you is _____

_____

_____

My favorite story that your parents tell about you is _____

_____

_____

_____

I remember when _____

_____

_____

The thing I like to do with you the most is _____

_____

_____

I always brag about _____

_____

I think you are like me because _____

_____

I love that you are different than I am about _____

_____

_____

You changed my life because _____

_____

I'd Like You to Know...

When I was young, I never guessed _____

_____

_____

My ambition has been _____

_____

_____

The thing I am most proud of in my life is _____

_____

I still wish I had _____

_____

Some events that left a lasting impression on me were _____

_____

_____

A turning point in my life was _____

_____

_____

Some of my ideals are _____

_____

_____

_____

I also value _____

_____

_____

_____

I hope I have instilled _____

_____

_____

_____

The most important thing I want to tell you is _____

_____

_____

_____

_____

_____

_____

What I Love about Our Family

The funniest story about our family is _____

_____

_____

_____

I still recall the time that _____

_____

I love it when we _____

I will never forget _____

_____

My biggest surprise was _____

I am so happy when we _____

_____

Our family is unique because _____

_____

_____

_____

In this photograph, _____

_____

(Place family photograph here)

Our Family Traditions

There are certain things our family does together that mean so much to me.
Here is what makes those times special...

Holiday _____

Our family celebrates by _____

On this day, we eat _____

I love this holiday because _____

_____

The first time you spent this holiday with the family, _____

_____

Holiday _____

Our family celebrates by _____

On this day, we eat _____

I love this holiday because _____

_____

The first time you spent this holiday with the family, _____

_____

Holiday _____

Our family celebrates by _____

On this day, we eat _____

I love this holiday because _____

_____

The first time you spent this holiday with the family, _____

_____

When someone in the family has a birthday, we _____

_____

_____

Another family celebration is _____

_____

Another tradition in our family is _____

_____

I started the family tradition of _____

_____

When I Was Your Age...

Times have changed, and so have I. It's fun to look back and see what the differences are.

The popular music was _____

My favorite singer was _____

My favorite actor was _____

My favorite actress was _____

The popular dance was _____

The fashion of the times was _____

The biggest fad was _____

My favorite family member was _____

My hobby was _____

I also enjoyed _____

I wasn't very good at _____

I got in trouble when _____

_____

Something that changed the world was _____

_____

My Wishes for the Future

My dream for you is _____

_____

For myself, I hope _____

_____

I wish that you and I _____

_____

I want our family to _____

_____

I can't wait until _____

_____

When you have a grandchild someday, I know _____

_____

And above all else, _____

_____

_____

_____

You and Me

*(Place photograph of your grandchild
and you here)*

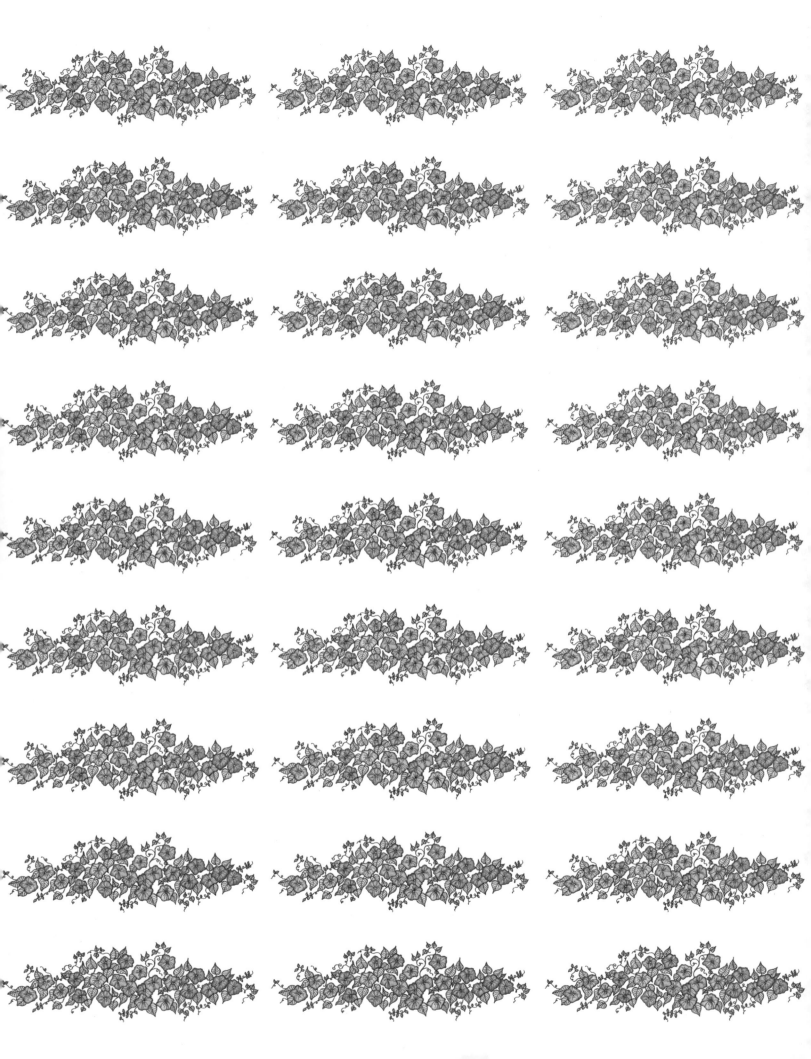